Selling The Million Dollar Model

by Dr. Lisa Marie Kennedy DC

Published by: Titan Marketing Solutions
316 Burland Avenue
Winnipeg Manitoba R2N 2T1
(204) 504-1866

DEDICATION

I dedicate this book to my father Delbert Brooks Burgess, who passed away right when I started writing the first chapter.

I would also like to dedicate it to my husband Matthew for always believing in me and my two daughters Brandi and Isabella, for being my driving force to succeed in life.

ACKNOWLEDGEMENTS

First, I must thank Grant Cardone for inspiring me to want more out of life, but more importantly, believing I can have it all. Thanks also to Ebong Eka for pouring power into me and knowing that this book would come to fruition. Danelle Delgado, Matt and Caleb Maddix for sharing their knowledge with me in St. Maarten and planting seeds inside me. They to believed, in me and showed me the steps to take to the next level. And finally, Paul Douglas for knowing he was the right fit for me and lighting a fire under me when needed.

FOREWORD
By Rob Anspach

How committed are you? That's the
question I want you to think about when
reading this book. Would you be committed
after losing your job? Or getting a divorce?
Or even moving to a new area? Not many
would. Yet, Lisa Kennedy smashes through
those barriers to bring you her life, her
experiences, her joys and her pains to
show you how it's all possible. And how to
stay committed to those beliefs and
dreams.

Without a plan of action, without mentors
and without support from your family,
selling real estate can be a downright
frustrating way to make a living. But if
you're committed to your dreams, then
Lisa's book can be your guide to fulfillment
in the million-dollar home market.

While Lisa was midway through writing
this book, I had the honor of interviewing

her through video chat. We talked about her branding and how her pink highlighted hair has become sort of her trademarked look. We talked about social media and how she's using it to build trust with her audience, and we talked about her goals and aspirations.

We also talked about hard life lessons and how overcoming those failures can have the greatest impact on your life. And she revealed what her next car would be once she achieved certain goals. What kind of car do you think she said? Would you like to know? I'll give you a hint, it starts with a "B".

All through this book, you'll discover how to implement those goals, what it means to be better than your competition and how to succeed where others have failed. You'll learn tricks, tips and strategies that will help you achieve higher sales and give you the edge needed to succeed in the real estate market.

So again, I ask you, how committed are

you?

For Lisa, it took years of determination and thousands of hours of sweat, tears and hard work to build her network. If you follow what Lisa shares in this phenomenal book, you'll cut your learning time in half and be on your way to being the authority in your market.

So, I challenge you to follow Lisa and learn from her, to go out and "crush it" and make a name for yourself...and to someday write your own book to inspire others and show the world your commitment.

Best wishes to your success.

Rob Anspach
Founder, Anspach Media
www.AnspachMedia.com

INTRODUCTION

I moved away from the freezing cold weather in South Portland, Maine when I turned 21 years old. The March wind was briskly blowing as I looked at my sweet mother's face. "I never thought you would go through with it", she said. She didn't believe me when I told her that I was moving to Florida.

As I packed the last of my assorted travel bags and trash bags into my 1985 red Ford Tempo, I felt empowered. We had never traveled much back then so trash bags seemed like a good option. I attempted to pack everything I owned because I knew I was never coming back.

Growing up, I never wanted for anything; I was an only child and my parents worked extremely hard with neither one of them having a high school diploma. My Mom earned her GED, worked at the hospital after having me at the age of 17 and my Dad was a laborer at B & M Baked Beans.

My father also had a part time gig cleaning bars on Sunday mornings when I was a teenager and I was able to master Pac-Man and Galaga and show off my skills when I went roller skating on the weekends. That was a huge deal. I wanted to be the best at everything I did.

WELCOME TO THE SUNSHINE STATE. I had never seen that sign before and it seemed to be the best thing I had set my eyes on in quite some time. Everything was coming together for me, whatever my 21-year-old mind was thinking, it was thinking BIG.

I had graduated cosmetology school and I had visions of being the hairstylist to the stars—Superstar status! I had my fair share of choices to work in Orlando and I had to find a place fast. I was living in a less than desirable apartment with no furnishings, sleeping on a blow-up bed and living on Raman noodles.

Yes, that is the only affordable option when you are flat broke. I landed a job in the Winter park mall but it didn't take long for me to realize that I had to get a second job and I needed cash like yesterday.

If you have ever been to Orlando, the number of restaurants is endless and with some waitressing experience, I knew I could find a job so I grabbed the paper.

"Hairstylist needed for dancers" is what I came across next.

How cool!

Doing hair for dancers-I called immediately and found out that it wasn't the type of dancer I thought. It was an adult entertainment establishment, doing hair and makeup for exotic dancers. I had never stepped foot into a strip club until I interviewed for the position that day in 1991.

Talk about making cash fast—this was the

place to be. Some days I made more than I did a whole week doing hair at the salon. There are many other details and events that happened during this time in my life but the point I'm trying to make here is that my brain has always worked in that fashion. How can I make the quickest money possible in the shortest amount of time? After some bad choices and life mistakes, I moved to Atlanta and started fresh in the year 1993.

I started college, bought my first house at the age of 26, got engaged…. then 4 years later it all fell apart. Fast forward to 2003 and I found myself at 33 years old living back home with my Mother in Maine at the lowest time of my life.

This was a turning point for many reasons. I was lonely, felt like a failure and had very few friends in Maine that understood what I was going through so it was during this time that I did some very deep soul searching.

I'm talking the kind of digging deep that

forces you to look in mirror and ask yourself some serious questions. Some of which, I didn't know the answer and sadly, some of the answers were painful.

I started reading and learning about manifesting the things in your life that you desire. I wrote down a list of qualities that I wanted in a husband. I was 33 years old and failed at many relationships so started writing my wish list.

I also started journaling/writing poetry and it was therapeutic for me. This is when I really started to believe in the law of attraction and slowly things started coming into my life. I was taking major action and got a new job with an orthopedic device company, then I landed a job with an animal diagnostics company and in the summer of 2013, I got my Florida real estate license and here I am today in 2016 sharing my journey with you.

There are many reasons why I wanted to share my story, but most of all, I want to help people. I want to help those that are struggling with circumstances that they think are impossible to overcome. What I have learned is that the situation you are in at this moment is just that, a moment. It can be changed with just one decision and that one decision can change your whole destiny.

"It is in your moments of decision that your destiny is shaped." - Tony Robbins.

ABOUT

This book encompasses many things.

Selling. Life. Challenges.
Buying. Financials. Luxury. The Not So Luxurious.
Most Importantly, Conquering Fear.

Table Of Contents

CHAPTER ONE

PREPARE

Roman philosopher, Seneca has been attributed with the quote, "Luck is what happens when preparation meets opportunity."

The first step to becoming a top producer and selling million-dollar real estate lies in your preparation. There is opportunity everywhere if you are prepared for it.

If you had asked me over ten years ago what I would be doing in 2016, I would not have said building a real estate empire, writing a book and overcoming my father's death.

Throughout my career in medical sales, I got to see firsthand the good, the bad and the ugly of corporate America and how it affected my mindset. I knew when I left that marketplace 4 years ago that I was never going back and that I was certainly not going to answer to another greedy CEO of a publicly held company.

I would not trade that experience for any price as it was invaluable to me in developing the skillset that I use every day selling million dollar homes. It has been said that you should work to learn instead of working to earn. I was fortunate in that I was able to do both with that career. Without that experience I would not have been as well prepared for my career in real estate.

In 2012, I was asked to relocate or accept a severance package. Leaving, or should I say being pushed out, was the single best thing that has happened to me professionally. I had learned all I could from that position and was ready to accept new challenges and opportunities for professional growth.

My severance package was decent, so as soon as I could collect it, I did. I decided to take the summer of 2012 off, with no plan other than to spend time with my two beautiful daughters for all of June and July.

I had felt a lot of guilt over the previous nine years, because of all the traveling with animal diagnostics taking me away from my family. I was a corporate slave, answering to the yes men of a clearly corrupt industry. I was living my life by quarters, and my family dreaded my presence at the end of every March, June, September and December. It was ultimately the demise of my relationship with the father of my children.

I was forbidden to take time off at Christmas - even if I was "at goal". There was always more expected of my team and me. It was high stress, I was a hot mess behind closed doors, my health suffered at times but the financial rewards and perks were outstanding.

There was one year I had earned a cruise

to Cabo. That very same year, I separated from the girls' father. We were never married, only engaged and could never get it quite right but remain a very close blended family today. We had already accepted, booked the trip and a month before the cruise, he left. This was undoubtedly one of the worst times in my life.

This situation left me feeling embarrassed, confused and it was an eye-opening trip that forced me to be on my own. I earned it and there was no way I was giving it up.

In 2011, I had earned another trip to Riviera Maya and Matthew (who is now my husband) and I had a beautiful time. He wasn't living in Florida and we were working the long-distance relationship so it worked out well.

Matthew and I went to high school together. We had reconnected and were dating long distance for over a year. It wasn't easy but we made it work and it was definitely nice to be able to go on a vacation together.

That same year, I knew I wanted something different. I had always dreamed of being an entrepreneur and no one ever showed me how. Looking back, I wish so badly that someone would have shoved Grant Cardone in my face.

Everything happened the way it was supposed to happen. I'm a big believer in the universe and that there are no coincidences, only intentions. All of what happened in these years was preparing me for the next move.

Good or bad, you are the sum total of all of your experiences in your life. Everything you have experienced has prepared you for this moment in time. It has prepared you for greatness.

It is now time for you to take the next step. You are ready. You have earned the opportunity that is now before you.

"I decided back in 2004 that my life was no longer going to be that of chance and wonder."

CHAPTER TWO

DECIDE

The year 2012 was a phenomenal year. Matthew and I were finally living together in Florida, the girls were growing and bonding with Matthew and we had finally found peace in our family with the girls' father. We had agreed that we would always be a blended family and never have to separate holidays.

Right around this same time we had kicked up our fitness challenges and in addition to all the mud runs we were doing, we decided to learn Krav Maga. This is an Israeli self-defense technique and pushed me to my ultimate fitness capabilities.

The following principles define krav maga: Strive for maximum versatility, defend and attack simultaneously, never assume that the fight is over, train from positions of disadvantage, target vulnerable areas, let reality dictate your response, use instinctive movements, train to build sound tactics and strive to get yourself as safe as possible as quickly as possible.

Krav maga's basic philosophy is aggression and threat neutralization, which are tenets that align well with the IDF Special Forces where Krav Maga is standard training. I was in the best shape of my life while training and went on to earn my Level 2 certification.

Our Krav Maga instructor at the time approached me after he learned I would be leaving my corporate position.

"So whatcha going to do now?"

I said I would continue to build my Visalus business (MLM) and take a couple months off.

He had his selfish reasons, but he did say to me...

"You should get your real estate license. Selling is selling, I'm starting a team and you would be a great real estate agent."

Two months later, there I was, real estate license in hand and working on a team at an international real estate brokerage.

It was an incredible amount of learning all at once. Fire hosed actually. He had a different way of doing things. He was extremely aggressive, dominant and never did business without a mandatory buyer's agent agreement. That is undeniably the best thing that I learned from him. The buyer's agreement is key.

The relationship dissolved quickly, within

a matter of 6 months, due to his lack of ethics and integrity. He ended up stealing from me and the brokerage and things did not end well for him. However, I do have to give him credit for encouraging me to get my license. There is always a silver lining in every story.

I went from the original brokerage to another broker and friend, and really learned how much there was to know, not just from a fundamental standpoint but also from a legal standpoint. There was so much knowledge that I had not been given in the beginning, I almost felt like I was starting over again.

I kept my eyes on the prize and all the successful agents. I had picked out a few that I wanted to emulate. I even wanted to pose like they did in their magazine shots. I was envisioning myself on the magazine cover and saw myself on TV showing the beautiful luxury properties of Sarasota, Siesta Key, Longboat Key and Lakewood Ranch.

It took about four months for me to finally sell my first home. It was a new construction build in Sarasota and I had been at numerous homes with this couple and never once did they mention new construction.

If you are a real estate agent or aspire to be, this is likely the most imperative thing to take note of, even if you stop reading right now. Remember this. Your buyers will go out without you, which is why the buyer's agreement is imperative to have signed.

What does this do?

It holds your buyer accountable to only work with you and it guarantees that you get paid. If I didn't have this document signed, I would have been slighted out of thousands of dollars. This was not a good experience for me or my buyers because of a situation that had happened with my so-called mentor.

I felt for my buyers because I wasn't

there when I should have been and I was very naive still. Limited knowledge and feeling very lost are the two terms that come to mind.

Matthew was extremely supportive and even encouraged me to go back to veterinary diagnostics sales. He knew it was a safe bet. I knew it was a safe bet. But I also knew I wouldn't be happy being safe.

In those few short months, I did what I wanted, when I wanted and for the first time in my life I was a 1099 (Earning self-employed income). What an amazing feeling. Risky, but I loved that feeling.

At this time, I decided to venture out and go to every networking event that I could go to. I met some fantastic people. What I realized that rarely would I see the big dogs. The super successful agents. I was seeing all the same faces.

What good was that?

I decided to get a bit more assertive and go to a Lakewood Ranch event at Country Club East. It was held at a John Cannon model. John Cannon is a builder I had heard of, but knew nothing about.

So, off I went.

I still remember what I was wearing that cold January morning. It's not very often that I get to wear boots in Florida. So, I marched right up those stairs and was determined to make progress and meet someone that could help me. I spoke to everyone in the room and quite frankly I received some strange looks like, "WTF is she doing here?"

Finally, I walked up to Mark. I simply asked the question, "What are you supposed to do at these things?"

We laughed and he proceeded to tell me that he had been to so many of them that it came second nature. We chatted for a bit and he stared at me and asked…

"Have you ever thought about doing new home sales?"

I knew that instant that my career path just changed. I say this because the day before I was Googling and researching new construction.

Like I said before, the universe is always watching. "If you want something and you put it out there, the universe conspires to make it happen." (The Alchemist).

I remember back in 2003 right after I left Atlanta. I wrote a list of all the qualities I wanted in a man. Let's just say that 2003 was a rock bottom year for me. It was in those moments of fear and not knowing what to do with the rest of my life, I knew God had a plan for me. When you are in a bad place, it is sometimes challenging to see.

I decided back in 2004 that my life was no longer going to be that of chance and wonder. I decided that while I was back living with my mother at the age of thirty-four that I would no longer be a victim of a party mindset.

I decided that I wanted more for myself. I decided that average was not where I wanted to be like over 50% of the population.

I decided and knew that I was the exception. Lastly, I decided that I was going to be exceptional. That greatness was within me... and off I went.

"If you want something and you put it out there, the universe conspires to make it happen." **The Alchemist,** Paulo Coelho

CHAPTER THREE

COMMIT

How committed are you?

I believe the word commitment is overused and underrated.

For most of my life, whenever I thought of the word commitment, I thought of being committed in a relationship. I have also committed to many other things in my life such as workout challenges, races, my family and several jobs in the past. Here's the thing about commitment ~ it's short-lived if you don't have a plan.

A quick Google search allowed me to come up with this...

Com·mit·ment
noun
1. the state or quality of being dedicated to a cause, activity, etc. "the company's commitment to quality"
2. Synonyms:
   dedication, devotion, allegiance, loyalty, faithfulness, fidelity "her commitment to her students"
3. An engagement or obligation that restricts freedom of action.

Point number 1.

When you commit yourself to your real estate business, think of it as the same way as you would a relationship. Whether it's a new love or marriage you have with that person, you become committed. For example, you are going to be married to this business through sickness and health. There are going to be days when you do not feel like getting out of bed. There will be days when you don't feel like performing at all but you do it anyway because that's what is needed. In a marriage or business, there are going to be days when it will feel like the universe is against you and these are the days that you should truly push to the fullest extent.

This commitment is what will make you the peak performer above all other agents in your area. This is why it's so important to write down your daily goals as a reminder of your commitment. Write down goals for every aspect of your life because they are all related. The reality is, if you are off in one area of your life, it will affect the other areas as well.

Family Goals=Business Goals=Spiritual Goals=Wealth Goals.

Write down and pursue your goals for EVERYTHING.

Point number 2:

It's important to tell the world how serious you are. Declaration of your commitment whether it be on social media, to your family, and to your friends is vital to your success. This, my friends, is accountability in its best form.

I remember when I first joined the MLM business and part of the initial challenge was to take a photo of yourself in a bathing suit before your 90-day physical challenge... What the what? I sucked it up and I did it anyway because I wanted to see results. And you'll see results by doing this no matter how painful it is.

It could potentially be embarrassing for you on your journey to success and you will have people doubt you, laugh at you and clearly say to you that it cannot be done. This is all part of the commitment process and through this process you will learn that all the environmental factors around you will become less important as you grow your business.

Think of the things once again that come to mind when you think COMMITMENT:

It could be a religion.

Devote your life.

Submit your soul.

Walk the path intended.

Obey.

The BEFORE is important.

YOUR past is important as part of your story.

You could think of your commitment in 90 day increments, then you can also think of it as monthly commitments or weekly commitments and then drill down to a daily commitment.

You dial into your mindset and you create focus.

You must reflect daily and write down your progress. Your WINS are an important part of your declaration process.

You submit to your commitment even if it takes an hour to recheck.

Picture this--You are a week into your commitment and you're not seeing any results, which is perfectly normal. It is hard to see progress when you are building a foundation. This is when you have to go back and reevaluate your goal and commitments.

Reset, whether that be Saturday or Sunday- these are the days where I typically try to reset because you don't want to try to reset on a Monday morning. Sometimes I will even reset my mind on a Friday because for Realtors, salespeople and business owners, it doesn't matter which day of the week it is. You need to be performing at your best when it is required and not just Monday mornings.

I remember my days in medical sales

where I would always have the Sunday blues starting at noon, dreading the Monday morning conference call. This is the mindset that you want to get out of if you're currently leaving a 9-to-5 job. Thinking about what lies ahead from Monday through Friday does not exist in the real estate world. You have to train your mind and think of every day as a new opportunity to sell or list a home.

Think about it this way. How do you feel the first day before going on vacation? The giddiness, the excitement, is all you can think of. You can hardly wait to get going.

This is the mindset that you need to start every day with. The very same excitement, enthusiasm and anticipation that something wonderful is going to happen on this day. You need to reset so you go into every day with that same mindset.

I remember a story I once heard about a young man, at a beach, that asked a body builder how he can develop the same physique as the bodybuilder. Instead of answering the young man's question, the bodybuilder grabbed him and dragged the young man into the ocean.

The young man struggled and resisted, yet was powerless as his head was forcibly held under the water. He pushed, he struggled, he fought, scratched and kicked.

The young man's heart was pounding. His lungs were burning. He was starting to get dizzy. He was certain he was about to die. With one final push using every last ounce of strength remaining, he pushed up against the body builder with what appeared to be super human strength.

As his head broke above the water, he gasped deeply as he inhaled the life-giving air his body so desperately needed. The body builder stood the young man up, held him steady and said...

"When your desire to have an amazing body is a strong as the desire you just had to breathe, then and only then will you be able to have a physique like mine."

When I heard this story, I sat back and reflected on every achievement in my life. It all started with an all-consuming desire.

It was never a wish. It was never a 'someday, maybe I will have this...' It was, 'I want this. I need to achieve this.' It was all I focused on.

The type of client that buys million dollar plus homes also have a different mindset than clients that buy two hundred and fifty thousand dollar homes. They want to work with someone that is committed. Someone who is playing all in. Someone who is committed to their career.

They are busy, and have high expectations and standards. If your expectations and standards are not on the same frequency as theirs, you will not attract their business. If you go into the relationship with your luxury clients halfheartedly and uncommitted, you are doing them a disservice.

Commit yourself to your career, to achieving your goals, to focusing on what needs to be done, even when you don't feel like doing it.

That is the level of commitment that you need to bring to the game if you want to sell the million-dollar model.

So, let me ask you again. How committed are you? Is your desire to sell a million-dollar home as strong as your desire to breathe? If it is, then congratulations, you are ready to move on to the fourth step.

"When your desire to have an amazing body is a strong as the desire you just had to just breathe, then and only then will you be able to have a physique like mine."

CHAPTER FOUR

TAKE ACTION

In the early 1990s, marketing guru Daniel S. Kennedy wrote a book called "The Ultimate Success Secret". The entire message of that book could have been distilled to two words. Care to guess what those two words are?

If your guess was "Take Action" you would be right.

It has always been my experience that even taking the wrong action is better than taking no action. With the wrong action, you can always correct your course with the feedback you receive. Conversely, when you fail to take action you are not moving forward or backwards. You are stagnant. There is no feedback. You are stuck.

After completing the Florida state exam for my real estate licensing, I felt like most agents do - overwhelmed and a bit lost. Although I was with a very large and popular brokerage, I didn't know where to start. I knew that prospecting was a very important component and something that I wasn't afraid of.

I had been cold calling my whole sales career so rejection was never an issue for me. I prepared, I decided and I was committed, now the next step was to take action. It took me a little bit of time to realize that not only do you have to take action you have to take a huge amount of action. This is where the 10x Rule by Grant Cardone comes into the picture.

In April 2014, a little app called Periscope launched and I found myself addicted to this live broadcasting phenomenon. I found Grant Cardone on Periscope and became infatuated with his message. He talked about having everything in life; having a super life actually.

Everything he spoke of, I just kept saying to myself "I want that! I want financial stability for my family, I want peace with my spirituality, I want the ultimate marriage and I wanted wealth." Not just in the financial sense but feeling wealthy in life!

"Anyone that suggests to me to do less is either not a real friend or very confused". Grant Cardone

My husband Matthew thought I was losing my mind because I was so consumed with this message of 10x.

The idea is to take all of your goals and every aspect of your life and simply multiply it times 10. Imagine putting 10 times the effort into everything you do on a daily basis.

I started this on a career level and really focused on making 100 calls per day. These calls were mostly follow up calls and were to prospects that had walked into the model home at one point or another.

There were many days where I did over 100 calls. I was finally some making headway. I had stacks of papers and everything was hand written because I did not have a CRM or a client relationship management system. A CRM is an invaluable tool where you can input your data and take notes, making it easier to keep track of your calling cycle.

Some people call it a list. I call it the engine which makes the vehicle run. Although I was able to multiply my efforts 10 times I still felt like I was running in circles because everything was manual. I decided at that point that I needed my own CRM and invested in the system and paid for it myself. It was worth the $25 per month to have a database of people that I had actually met face-to-face. Within six months' time I had over 400 names, emails and phone numbers.

For any agent just starting out in real estate, I would say that this is the single most important tool that you will need to take action. This is a fabulous tool if you are doing open houses, as you can input all of your data and have it at your fingertips. Many systems offer capabilities much more than just client data but this is a great starting point.

In my personal life, I knew that if I could multiply my efforts in my relationship that I would see results in that, as well as in my career. I changed my whole mindset towards my relationship and I refused to give up as I had in past relationships. Matthew and I were not yet married but he had proposed to me two weeks after I started my job with the design build firm.

I wanted the ultimate marriage and I was willing to put in the work. I wrote down all of my goals for a relationship and shared them with him. It was challenging at first because my mindset was changing, and I expected his to do the same. No fault of his however, he wasn't as open-minded as I expected he would be.

Over time I started realizing that just because I had adopted a certain mindset didn't mean that he had or that I had the right to force it upon him. When you're in this process self-awareness is hugely important and the expectations that you have of others needs to be thrown out the window. Just because I had come across something life-changing I didn't mean that he felt the same way.

You can only control you, and your mindset.

So, what can you 10X in your life? Your career? Your relationships?

Over ninety per cent of success is in showing up. While everyone else is waiting for opportunity to knock on their door, you can go out and create your own opportunity, simply by taking massive action.

What I want you to do before going to chapter five is to take action. Divide a sheet of paper into five columns. At the top of each column, I want you to write down the headings, Health, Wealth, Relationships, Spirituality, and Happiness.

In each column, write down the one activity that if you 10Xed it, you would experience exponential growth and results.

"Anyone that suggests to me to do less is either not a real friend or very confused."
Grant Cardone

CHAPTER FIVE

GET ATTENTION

When most people think of taking action, they think of doing certain things and taking steps to do it. What I learned from Grant Cardone from the 10x rule is that you take your goals and you multiply them by 10. So, if my goal is making 10 calls that day, instead I would make 100 phone calls. This type of action on a consistent basis will put you way ahead of everybody else in your game.

Taking action also meant that I had to put myself out there on live broadcast and platforms. In January 2016 I was a guest on one of my friends shows on Periscope, shortly after that first episode he called and told me that the current executive producer could no longer do the showing; would I be interested? I happily obliged and that show was a huge success for 42 weeks. I then decided that the show was not aligned with the bigger calls that I had for my future. This part is challenging because there will be some things that you don't necessarily want to give up, but if it doesn't serve you in the correct way you have to let it go. I accomplished the task of getting known because everyone associated me with live broadcasting, so I was getting attention and I was taking massive action towards reaching the major influencers.

During that time, I also just started Snapchatting on a regular basis... 15 to 20 Snaps per day and gradually adding influencers and like-minded people to my Snapchat feed. This is a great way to engage other real estate agents in different parts of the country and also keep up on the market trends. People want to see what you are doing in your personal life as well as your business life, so you have to find a way to mix the two together that you feel comfortable with. Doing videos on Instagram was extremely successful for me and still continues to be because you can share it with your public Facebook page. All these types of actions are designed to get you out there and get you known.

Moving with speed is crucial. We live in such a lackadaisical world today and everyone thinks that they are busy but when you tear the onion peel apart you'll see that they are exactly that - just busy and not truly productive. Most are not doing tasks that will move them forward to their goals. If you walked into any real estate office today, let's take an office that has maybe 200 agents, there may only be 15 to 20 agents actually being productive in that office. Sure, there may be some agents out showing property, but a large majority of them are either working from home or not really putting their everything into building a business or a team for that matter.

Tony Robbins created a system he calls MAP, which is the acronym for Massive Action Plan.

Once you have absolute clarity about the exact result you want and why you must achieve it, the next step is to create the MAP (Massive Action Plan) to get yourself there. Using a MAP goes beyond goal setting; it changes the emotional meaning behind all of your activities and forms a stronger link back to the outcome, making it more likely you'll achieve it.

When you're creating your MAP, ask yourself, "How much?", "By when?" and "For what purpose?" Then write it down. Make it a permanent, tangible expression of your mental target.

Exercise: Are you committed to make a change? Complete your own Massive Action Plan in the graphic below to help you stay on track.

Write down the results you want to achieve.

Write down your purpose (compelling reasons why you want to accomplish your goals).

Develop a sequence of priority actions.

I'm not reinventing the wheel here only implementing what has already been done by very successful people.

Moving with speed is crucial.

CHAPTER SIX

CREATE VALUE

Would you like the ultimate secret to zero resistance sales?

Here it is.

Make sure the real and perceived value of your product far exceeds your asking price. When you can do that, resistance melts away, and selling the million-dollar model becomes so much easier.

Want to eliminate all competition?

Provide massive upfront value, with no strings attached.

Price is what you pay. Value is what you get. This is where the magic happens. If you were to read any article today about social media influencing, the first thing people talk about is giving value first.

The question is, in a huge cesspool of marketing messages, information and different social media platforms, how do you actually set yourself apart from all that noise? You create the value that your marketplace needs. The purpose of selling your value is to interpret the value of your solution to the client.

Let's go ahead and take a very, very familiar situation that I'm often confronted with. A lovely couple walks into my $1.75 million home. The first thing I want them to know is that they are going to get great value when they buy from me. So, my first mission is to get them to know me, like me and trust me. I do this by asking questions that will lead into agreeing about their needs. Most people that buy a home in this price range don't really need a house. You find out their story and you realize that it is their emotions that are driving them towards this purchase, not the actual dwelling.

I often ask questions like who, what, where, when, how. I know that seems very simple but so many real estate agents are confused about the sales process because most never really took the time to take a sales class, so they just want to tell them about the house before they even know why their client wants the house.

Once you find out their pain and emotions, you can work around that, then you can dig into the features, functions, and benefits. Once you've tied that all together and agreed on the needs, you may even want to provide some evidence such as a third-party reference or personal testimony. In most cases if you have created enough value, the customer is going to convince themselves.

Example: 'Mrs. Hopps, you'll really love the insulated impact glass windows and doors.' (feature). 'They will allow for much better energy efficiency.' (function) 'and there will be no need for hurricane shutters.' (benefit).

This very next step is one that salespeople in every industry miss the mark on and that is simply asking for the order! This is the sole purpose of reaching closure and solving the customer's problem. This is a win-win situation because if the answer is, 'Yes I will buy your product,' you've achieved your goal. If the answer is no, there will most likely be an objection that follows behind it, and you can tackle that objection if you've asked the right questions in the beginning.

Here are some examples of mini closes that you could use along the way in the selling process. These mini closes will help to create value because it essentially means that they have agreed with you on their pain points and you feel their pain.

*When would be the best time to start?
*Since you've agreed to XYZ, I will go get the paperwork for your review.

If we agree on the plan and on the price, are you ready to move forward?

And the ultimate close: 'Great, Mrs. Hopps, sign here and let's get started!'

You have officially solved their problem and created value at the same time.

Provide massive upfront value, with no strings attached.

CHAPTER SEVEN

NON CONFORMING

As I write this next chapter Mr. Donald Trump has just been elected 45th president of the United States of America. This is a perfect example of non-conforming nature.

Many of his statements in interviews, on Twitter, and at campaign rallies have been controversial and in my opinion, he displays nonconforming actions. I look at this at non-conforming behavior as one that separates him from many other past presidents.

He is currently the chairman and president of The Trump Organization, the principal holding company for his real estate ventures and other business interests – a position he has said he will vacate prior to his attainment of the presidency. During his career, Trump has built office towers, hotels, casinos, golf courses, and other branded facilities worldwide.

Love him or hate him, never in the history of America have we had a president like this. He does not conform to a generally accepted pattern of thought or action. This is exactly what I want to talk about in the real estate world.

Whether you're transitioning from another career or just starting out in your real estate career, it is imperative that you do not follow or listen to those who have not done what you seek to do.

The opinions of others on the real estate industry are skewed at best. While non-conforming terminology can be used in the real estate vocabulary, I am referring to your personal relationship with the nonconforming idea.

Have you ever had a great idea and then verbalized it to your friends and family and then been shot down? Get used to this. You have to be willing to put a wall up against opinions that do not serve your purpose no matter who that person might be.

I mentioned earlier that when I transitioned out of medical sales that many people around me thought that it was a "risk" to delve into another career. Quite frankly, this is my fourth career change of my life and every single one of those choices have led me further down the path of success.

The way that I define it is - Society has always been comfortable with going to college, going into a field that you stand for the rest of your life, then retiring. The question that you have to ask yourself is, "does this make me happy every single morning when I get up and open my eyes?"

I have had many struggles with this and I can tell you that at the age of 46, if you're not excited to get out of bed at four or 5 AM in the morning, you're in the wrong career.

I just recently met someone that had a lifelong career in a certain field. She talked about how passionate she was about it and after a couple hours of conversation, turns out that she's passionate about it, but it wasn't really what she wanted to do. You can be passionate about something but not necessarily devote 40 to 50 hours a week of your life to it. I especially say this because if you're devoting that much time to it and you're working for somebody else is it really passionate for you?

This is where you should choose to non-conform. Choosing your heart about something passionate is very different from working for someone in a passionate field.

Does that make sense?

When you go back to the definition of non-conforming, it actually states "in accordance with success in a certain company. ".

Remember, when you get your real estate license, you may be with a broker, but you are 100% commission and all of that falls on your shoulders. You're just hanging your license with someone for the brand recognition or possibly for a team affiliation.

You are now a business owner and you cannot conform to any ideas or rules of anyone else other than your own when it comes to success principles. You may have to depending on the brand, but when you look at your financials, hire a bookkeeper and speak to your accountant you'll understand that non-conforming is the ultimate way to roll in real estate.

People underestimate the work that it takes to be successful in the real estate industry. They do not foresee the criticism that you will receive when you make choices that go against the grain. You have to accept the label and be the exception to the standard agent.

People underestimate the work that it takes to be successful.

CHAPTER EIGHT

FIND THE RIGHT PEOPLE

This step will be vital to your career. Finding the right people doesn't always mean that you have to find the ones in your industry. There are many things that you can learn from successful people just by doing a YouTube search. For example, when you type in "motivation tips", you will get everything from top life hacks, to the top 8 tips to work out and hundreds of other videos that you can learn from and in the process, find people that you can subscribe to on a regular basis.

I personally thought that my original mentor in real estate was the be-all end-all when I first started. I learned after a few months that it was not the solution. Joining a team is a great idea, for some people that are just getting started. You have to be willing to learn and sacrifice some of your income if you choose this scenario. There is really an endless amount of content on the Internet and even at local events, such as your realtor association in your city or town. The key to starting off on the right foot is finding the people that emulate what you want to be. There were very few in my city that actually were willing to help or that offered any value.

And that leads me to my next big topic, which is really going outside of your industry and finding a successful coach and mentor that you pay for. Yes, you will have to pay for a coach in business to get you to the next level. Let me say that one more time. You will have to pay for a coach, to get you to the next level. I'm sure you're sitting there now saying I thought I was going to learn everything as I went along. It doesn't happen seamlessly if you want to be the big dog. Sure, success does happen to some people that know the right people. For example, if you're just becoming a real estate agent and your husband happens to own a mortgage business that might be in your benefit, but the majority of people who get their real estate license have no connections whatsoever and are really starting from scratch.

When I talk about finding a coach I talk about investing, which is the next chapter but I can tell you right now my life and my finances did not change until I invested 10% of my annual income into self-development.

When you do this, you want to tell the world, you want to put it out on social media, on every single outlet that you have. You want to do this because you want to attract attention and make people wonder why you're doing what you're doing. I can't tell you how many times people have asked me "I saw your photos on Facebook, what was that?" They see that you've invested and they see the familiar faces in photos that you have with social influencers, not just in the market but social influencers in the entrepreneurial world. When people see this, they want to be a part of it, they want to know the secrets of success. I cannot tell you how many messages I received earlier on in 2015 about the photos that I had and how did I get them or how did I know these people. It is the power of connecting with people that have the same interests as you. It is the power of social media. It is the power of reaching out to influencers. There is power in numbers and when you have large numbers of people that are influencers you then become an influencer as well. Find the right people to connect with and you will build your path.

"I am the person, this is the place and this is the right time to connect with the right people".

Here is my recommendation when it comes to coaches. You will reach a point where they have helped you as much as they can. You will need to move on to the next coach when that happens.

Just like when you were a kid in school. You would spend an entire school year with your coach (teacher). At the end of the school year, if you learned all you could from your coach, you moved on to the next level and a new coach. It is a natural progression.

"I am the person, this is the place and this is the right time to connect with the right people".

CHAPTER NINE

GET THE TOOLS

If you have read this far then you have already have committed yourself to the career of being an entrepreneur in real estate.

I remember hearing a very good analogy about abundance. Abundance is like the ocean. It is limitless and always regenerating itself. It will never run out. It can never be depleted.

With this ocean of abundance, you can go to the shore and take from it all you want. Some people will go down with a thimble and take very little, while others will go down with buckets. Some enterprising individuals are willing to put in additional effort and divert a small stream of abundance to them. Fewer still will set up a pumping station so they can continuously send abundance to them.

Originally this moral of this tale is that abundance does not care how much you take, it will always give you what you ask as it is not in short supply.

I look at it from a different perspective. The greatest abundance in this story went to those that had the best tools. That is why in this chapter I want to share with you the tools I use aside from the obvious phone/laptop to sell the million-dollar model.

Here is the list of the tools I use daily.

1. Goal setting planner - long term, short term. You would think this would be an obvious one.
2. Vision board- you don't know where you're going unless you have a vision.
3. CRM - Client Relationship Management System.
4. MLS System.
5. Website.
6. Local Association Education Events.
7. Chamber of Commerce
8. BNI Associations
9. The Internet

Let's talk about why these tools are important if you want to sell the million-dollar model.

I ranked my goal setting planner as my most essential tool. It is how I stay on track, stay committed, and most importantly, how I keep score. So much has been written about setting goals that I won't go into it here.

What I will cover is why you need to have your goal planner.

I have written down in my planner my long term, two- to five - year goals. Each of my long-term goals have then been reverse engineered into my short term goals, which in turn have been reversed into my daily action plans.

How do you eat an elephant? One bite at a time. For many people, they often don't chase bigger dreams as they can get overwhelmed by the enormity of it, so they temper it down to what they feel are realistic.

By breaking your big, hairy, audacious goals down into bite sized daily actions, you will be surprised how simple and easy it is to transform and achieve your biggest goals.

A vision board is another invaluable tool I have. It is what keeps me focused and motivated. There really are no rules to creating a vision board except one. It must speak to you.

So, what will you find on my vision board? You will see pictures of my husband and daughters. A Disney Cruise ship. My next car. The bank balance I want to see at the end of the year. Pictures of mentors and influencers I need to meet and work with to name a few.

Now here is the most important part. You need to place your vision board where you will see it several times a day. The bathroom, your office, your home office, even the background wallpaper on your computer.

As I mentioned in an earlier chapter, things didn't turn around for me until I implemented a CRM (customer relationship management) tool to track my leads and prospects. I will discuss CRMs in more detail in the next chapter.

You will also need a website. There are lots of options out there for you. If you are starting out and broke, you can create a simple site using WIX. It is free to build a simple site. Your brokerage may also offer you a replicated corporate site.

The downside to these options is that they rarely if ever rank well in the search engines. The second challenge, at least in my case is that I am not a digital marketer. So putting up a DIY website and hoping to compete would be like my taking on a MMA fighter with the little bit of Krav Maga training I have. I may get lucky, but realistically I am going to get my butt kicked.

In my case I chose to hire a digital marketer to build my websites, produce videos, create my Facebook ad campaigns, and even helped me with this book you are reading.

The next three tools - Attending your local association events, being an active member of your chamber of commerce, and BNI - all fall under networking. Networking can be a very powerful way to connect with other people and develop relationships. However, you need to be very selective where you network. It is so easy to go to networking events, leads clubs, mixers, and meetups that you start to believe you are productively growing your business. I have met people at these events that invest 20, 30 even 40 hours or more per week going to networking events. I am left wondering if they are using it as a way to avoid what needs to be done to produce a sale.

Hold every event accountable. These are not social clubs. You are there to get known, create relationships, and build trust so that the people you meet would be happy to work with you if they need to buy or sell a home, or refer you to someone that needs your help.

So work these events smart. That means don't run around, handing out your business card to everyone that can fog a mirror. Don't beg people for referrals. We have all seen that individual at networking events and there is nothing more pitiful.

Don't talk about your business. Invest that time connecting to the people you meet. Be sincerely interested in them and their business. Find out what keeps them up at night, find out who their ideal client is, who they want to meet. Then do what you can to send them a highly-qualified referral afterward.

Here is a ninja tip for you. After the event, connect with them on LinkedIn.

Finally, you need to be online. There is so much free content out there these days. I can't tell you how many free e-books I've downloaded in the past year. You want to make sure you have a mix of real estate motivation and inspiration. You're going to need all of three of these things to feed your soul. Sometimes the journey in real estate is a lonely one and you're going to need to stay motivated.

Are there more tools? Yes. You will find them in the next chapter.

*"How do you eat an elephant?
One bite at a time."*

CHAPTER TEN

AUTOMATE YOUR PROCESS

In the last chapter I spoke of the tools I use daily to manage both my business and my lead flow. Now I want to talk to you about automating these processes so that you have remote control systems in place so you can focus on your most profitable activities.

A word of caution before we proceed. A lot of the products I am about to share are subscription based, require some technical expertise to utilize, and may have a vertical learning curve that makes you feel as if you slammed into a brick wall.

Subscription based tools add up fast to a large monthly expenditure. If you are going to invest in a tool, you need to ensure two things. One, use it. That should go without saying, but you would be surprised, I made a purchase with good intentions of following through and implementing its use, only to have life get in the way, get distracted, put out fires and forget all about it.

The second thing you need to ensure is do you really need it at this stage of your business. If you are making 10 calls a day then index cards and a plastic box would be a sufficient CRM for your needs. If you decide to 10X your business as I mentioned in chapter four, then you will need something a little more robust.

There are three extremely important areas of your business that you would need to automate. They are accounting, customer management and follow up, and social media.

Let's start with accounting. The reality is, if we were good at accounting, we would most likely be accountants and not selling million-dollar real estate. Yet we still need to accurately record and report our income and expenses in order to avoid the hefty fines and penalties that the IRS can impose upon you. Lack of organization on your part can cost you thousands of dollars. Dumping a shoebox full of receipts and cancelled checks onto your accountant's desk is a great way to get fired by that same accountant. There are a number of cloud based products out there that you can use. The two biggest ones that come to mind are QuickBooks and FreshBooks. My preference is for QuickBooks.

When evaluating a cloud accounting package, you want to measure against the following criteria. How many users can you create? The more users you have the higher your subscription fee. The very minimum user accounts you should have are three users, One for yourself, and the other two for both your bookkeeper and accountant. As you grow you will want to scale it as you add user accounts for your support staff. You will also want an app for your phone and tablet. It can be difficult to remember to enter a gas or lunch receipt at the end of the day. Snapping a picture of your receipt and assigning it to an expense account is simple, quick and easy. Finally, make sure the accounting package you choose offers full support. Whether it is answering an accounting or tax question, resetting your forgotten password, or even a full professional setup, the support offered should also be considered. As for subscription fees, most are priced between twenty to thirty dollars per month. That is less than a dollar a day to accurately track the financial side of your business.

Once you have your financial house in order, you now need to track and manage your customer flow and how you follow up with them.

A CRM will come to be your most valuable tool in your business. When setup properly, your CRM will allow you to record pertinent information such as your customers' needs, wants and wish lists, their timelines, careers, birthdays, and other special events. The CRM will also schedule your follow up calls, push out your follow up emails, and remind you as to when you need to send out a targeted mailing. The more advanced products will also allow you to segment your prospect list. That way you can send a very targeted offer to someone that is qualified for that offer. The very best way to have someone remove themselves from your marketing funnel is to send a prospect qualified for one point five million a listing for three million. Segmenting your list effectively prevents costly blunders like this.

I have used two CRMs in my career. When I first started out, I invested in InfusionSoft. In my opinion, it is the best of the best when it comes to automating your business, as it replaces several automation tools and easily integrates with other software.

The downside to InfusionSoft is its complexity and cost. There is a reason why so many people have nicknamed it ConfusionSoft. However, if you are willing to invest the time and money to master this product, or delegate a team member to using it, you will not find a better weapon to have in your automation arsenal.

The other CRM I have used is Base. It was provided to us by the luxury builder I work for. What I love about Base is the flexibility it offers me. Being cloud based and mobile, I can follow up with my prospects while I am sitting in the stands during my daughters' soccer games. It is not as pricey as InfusionSoft, but if I want to meet the functionality that InfusionSoft offers, I need to add modules to it. The other thing you will need to add if the CRM you select does not have an autoresponder integrated with it is an autoresponder. An autoresponder is a bulk email and list management tool. You never want to send bulk emails from your computer. ISPs have bulk email limits set to prevent spam.

Sending follow up emails out to people one at a time is both time consuming and inefficient, particularly if you are sending out invitations to an open house and you have a large list.

There are several autoresponder services out there. You can choose MailChimp, Aweber, Get Response, Constant Contact, and Instant Customer to name a few. For my websites, I use MailChimp.

The last automation tool is for social media. I have new real estate agents ask me all the time how I manage my social media. Truthfully, although there are several auto posting tools available, I am not a fan. I will share what I do in a moment.

For me, connecting with my followers should be authentic and real. Putting out a message just for the sake of it is nothing more than spam. Social media is far more manageable when you are not trying to be on all channels at the same time.

Pick the channels that are most relevant to you and your business. In my case, it is Facebook, followed by Snapchat, Instagram, Pinterest and Twitter. Facebook Live has now replaced Periscope as my go-to livestreaming tool. With Facebook, I can schedule posts to go out over the month and they automatically syndicate to Twitter. I can share an image on Instagram, which immediately gets shared on Facebook and then on Twitter. I have my accounts interlinked so I can share my content over a much broader audience.

In addition to scheduling my posts to go out over the month, I do spend some time everyday connecting with friends and followers. It allows me to be real, to be a part of the conversation, and to show them they are not connecting to a bot but the real me.

One last note about automation. It can save you a lot of time and put your business on remote control, freeing you up to focus on selling the million dollar models. Before you automate though, make sure you already have a system in place. Otherwise, you may find yourself with a costly monthly subscription sitting on your computer, tablet and phone doing nothing to help you grow your business.

"Before you automate though, make sure you already have a system in place."

CHAPTER ELEVEN

YOUR NEXT STEP

This book has been the first step on your journey to selling million dollar homes. Don't allow it to be your last. I have found that success in life can be boiled down to a series of sequential steps that move you ever closer to your goal.

So far, you have managed to follow me down the rabbit hole this far on your journey to selling million-dollar real estate.

So, what's next?

It is now time to look at the lessons espoused in this book and apply them to your business. Start with the foundational steps covered in the first three chapters. Prepare yourself to be a million-dollar producer. You must truly believe that not only are you capable of selling million dollar homes, but that you are actually qualified and deserve to sell these homes. Look back over your life experiences. The most challenging and painful experiences in your life have forged you into the person you are today. It is these experiences that have prepared you to be a million-dollar producer.

Decide to sell million dollar homes. All too often we have this feeling that we need to have others bestow our credentials upon us. You will wait a very long time to have others recognize your expertise. Other real estate agents believe they must work up to the million dollar homes by starting with homes priced at $250 000 or less. After a couple of years, they may move to homes under 500K. Then 750 and then they make the jump to the million-dollar club.

I am here to tell you that the way to earn the right to sell million dollar homes is to go out and sell a million-dollar home. You may never work your way up to sell million dollar homes if you never decide to do it. Make that decision now. Now commit to being someone that only works with million dollar homes. Set your standard and stick to it. Let it be known that you will only take on the best clients, and the best listings in the best neighborhoods.

Never, ever waver from your commitment because things may be tight financially. Broke is always a temporary state. Stick to your guns. You can create a small second income stream by sharing leads and listings with other agents in your office that haven't read this book. Just ask for a small finder's fee. It is also a great way to screen future team members. The most important thing you can do now is to take action. Implement the steps I have outlined in this book. I have often said that even the wrong action is better than inaction. When you take action, even the wrong action, you are working forward towards your goals. With inaction, you are stuck, stagnant and moving away from your goal.

So, go to that networking event, hire your web designer, take that continuing education course, subscribe to Grant Cardone's Cardone University, make those cold calls, and meet people. You will accomplish more through movement than you ever will through meditation.

So, get started. Now.

This is the one thing that if you do nothing else outlined in this book that will position you above your complacent peers.

Finally, I invite you to take your next step with likeminded entrepreneurs and myself. You finished this book. You took action.

I have created an exclusive private Facebook group for our readers to network with and go to for help and support. It is free to join and available only to those who have bought this book.

To get the link, go to http://sellingthemilliondolarmodel.com and click the members link to join.

I will see you on the inside.